THE NHL: HISTORY AND HEROES

TORONTO
MAPLE LEAFS

Published by Creative Education
P.O. Box 227, Mankato, Minnesota 56002
Creative Education is an imprint of The Creative Company.

DESIGN AND PRODUCTION BY **ZENO DESIGN**

Printed in the United States of America

PHOTOGRAPHS BY Corbis Bettmann, (JP MOCZULSKI/Reuters), Getty Images (Denis Brodeur/NHLI, Bruce Bennett Studios, Chris Cheadle, Mark Hicks, Hulton Archive, Gjon Mili//Time Life Pictures, Paul Nodler//Time Life Pictures, Dave Sandford, Ezra Shaw/NHLI, Ron Turenne/NBAE), Hockey Hall of Fame (Imperial Oil-Turofsky)

LIBRARY OF CONGRESS CATALOGING-IN-PUBLICATION DATA

McAuliffe, Bill.
The story of the Toronto Maple Leafs / by Bill McAuliffe.
p. cm. — (The NHL: history and heroes)
Includes index
ISBN 978-1-58341-621-1
1. Toronto Maple Leafs (Hockey team)—History—Juvenile Literature. I. Title.

GV848.T6M33 2008
796.962'6409713541—dc22   2007014999

First Edition

9 8 7 6 5 4 3 2 1

COVER: Center Mats Sundin

BILL McAULIFFE

THE NHL: HISTORY AND HEROES

CREATIVE ☾ EDUCATION

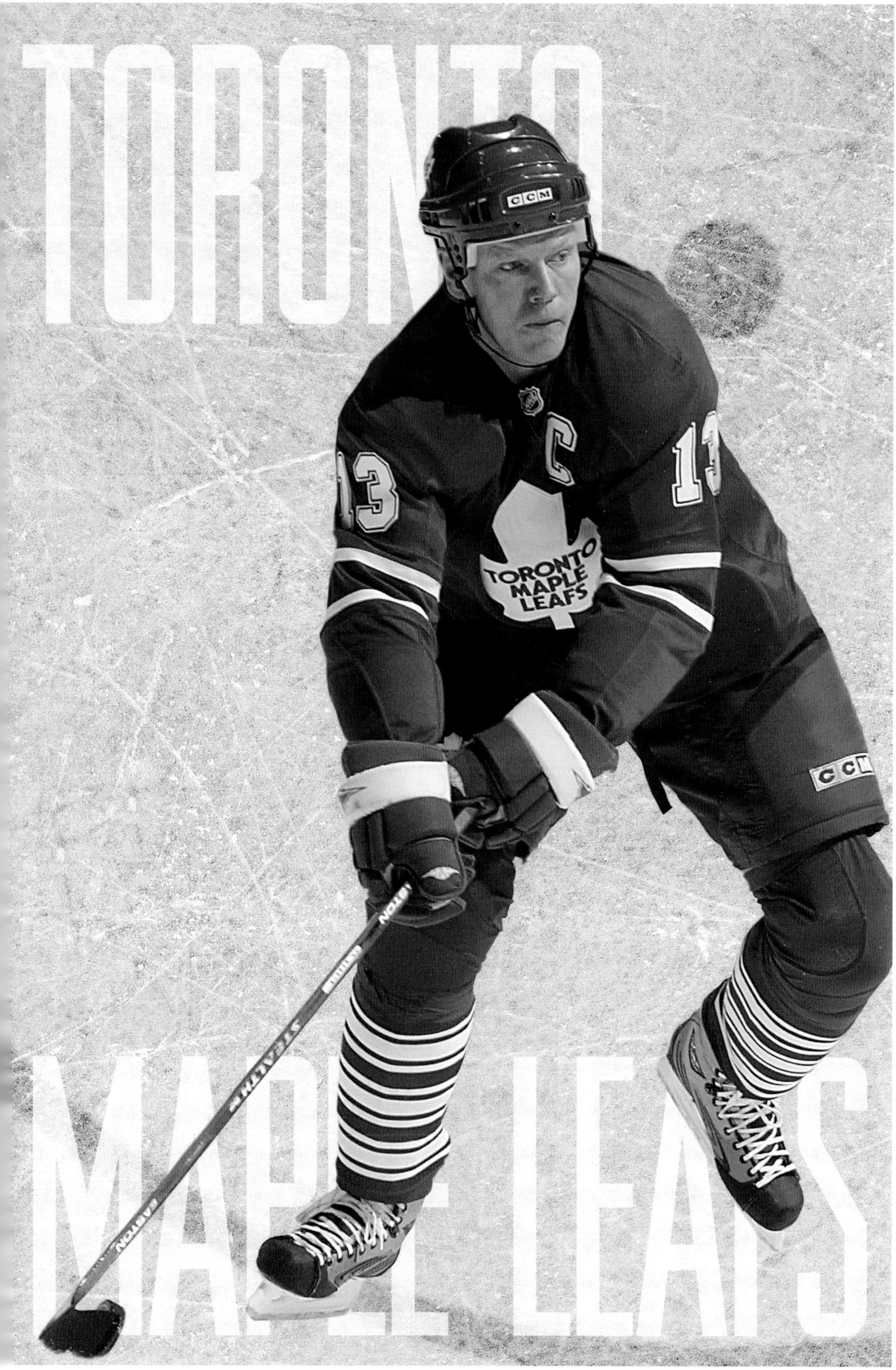
TORONTO
MAPLE LEAFS

BY THE TIME THE 2002 NHL PLAYOFFS BEGAN, IT HAD BEEN 35 YEARS SINCE THE TORONTO MAPLE LEAFS HAD WON A STANLEY CUP CHAMPIONSHIP. ANOTHER QUICK PLAYOFF EXIT SEEMED LIKELY, AS TORONTO WAS CRIPPLED BY IN-JURIES. STAR CENTER AND CAPTAIN MATS SUNDIN WAS OUT WITH A BROKEN WRIST, AND EVEN LEAFS COACH PAT QUINN WAS HOSPITALIZED WITH HEART PROBLEMS. BUT PLAYING WITH A DETERMINATION THAT MADE THE CROWDS INSIDE TORONTO'S AIR CANADA CENTRE BOTH LOUD AND PROUD, THE LEAFS EMBARKED ON ONE OF THE MOST MEM-

MAPLE LEAFS

ORABLE POSTSEASON RUNS IN THEIR 90-YEAR HISTORY. FIRST, THEY BROUGHT DOWN THE NEW YORK ISLANDERS IN SEVEN HOTLY CONTESTED GAMES. THEN, THEY OUTLASTED THEIR PROVINCIAL RIVALS, THE OTTAWA SENATORS, IN AN-OTHER SEVEN-GAME SERIES, CAPTURING THE LAST TWO GAMES. AND EVEN THOUGH THE MAPLE LEAFS CAME UP TWO VICTORIES SHORT OF THE STANLEY CUP FINALS, LOS-ING TO THE CAROLINA HURRICANES IN THE CONFERENCE FI-NALS, THE TORONTO FAITHFUL WERE LEFT BELIEVING THAT THAT ELUSIVE 14TH STANLEY CUP WOULD SOON BE THEIRS.

BLUE TO GREEN TO BLUE

ORIGINALLY A FUR-TRADING POST ON THE
shores of Lake Ontario, the city of Toronto, Ontario,
was established by British colonists in 1793. Today,
it is Canada's largest city, home to two and a half
million people and one of the world's tallest build-
ings, the 1,815-foot (553 m) CN Tower. Its downtown
also features the beginning of Yonge Street, which
has been called the world's longest street, running
1,178 miles from Lake Ontario to Ontario's border
with Minnesota.

For the last century, one of Toronto's best-known
enterprises has been its National Hockey League
(NHL) team, the Maple Leafs. The Leafs started out
in 1912 as a team called the Toronto Blueshirts of the

Founded more than two centuries ago, Toronto has grown rapidly since the mid-1900s and is today the fifth-most populous city in North America.

National Hockey Association (NHA), a league that started in 1910. In 1917, most of the NHA's teams formed the NHL, and the Toronto club—known that season as both the Blueshirts and the Arenas—won the 1918 Stanley Cup as world champions. Four years later, wearing green sweaters and known as the St. Patricks, the team won another. Then, Conn Smythe entered the picture.

Smythe had been a hockey star at the University of Toronto and was a decorated World War I veteran. He found success in the sand and gravel business, but his heart remained in hockey. In 1927, he bought the St. Patricks and named himself coach and general manager. Smythe soon changed the team's colors back to the blue and white he had worn at the University of Toronto. And in a show of patriotism, he adopted Canada's national symbol as the team logo. The club became the Toronto Maple Leafs, and Smythe set out to fill his roster with players that combined skill with toughness. "If you can't beat 'em in the alley, you can't beat 'em on the ice," he liked to say.

Darryl Sittler CENTER

Darryl Sittler, the Leafs' all-time leading scorer, arrived at Maple Leaf Gardens in 1970 and became a fan favorite during 12 years with the struggling team. He posted an NHL-record six goals and four assists in a 1976 game against the Boston Bruins, becoming the first player ever to score hat tricks (three goals) in successive periods. In that season's playoffs, he scored five goals in a game against the Philadelphia Flyers, tying another NHL record. In September 1976, he netted an overtime goal to win the Canada Cup for team Canada, cementing his status as a hockey hero in his native country.

MAPLE LEAFS SEASONS: 1970–1982
HEIGHT: 6-0 (183 cm)
WEIGHT: 190 (86 kg)

- 1,121 career points
- 18 career hat tricks
- 4-time All-Star
- Hockey Hall of Fame inductee (1989)

Playing pivotal roles as team founder, owner, coach, and general manager, Conn Smythe (left) was the face of the Maple Leafs franchise for decades.

Toronto wing Ace Bailey led the NHL in points (goals plus assists) in 1928–29, and the Leafs earned fame with their talented "Kid Line," a trio that featured center Joe Primeau and wings Charlie Conacher and Harvey "Busher" Jackson. In 1930, Smythe signed future Hall-of-Famer Francis "King" Clancy to play defense alongside standout Clarence "Hap" Day.

As he built his team, Smythe also organized and financed the construction of Maple Leaf Gardens, which opened on November 12, 1931. That year, he remained general manager but turned the coaching reins over to Dick Irvin. After finishing second in the Canadian Division, one of the NHL's two divisions, the 1931–32 Maple Leafs slipped past the Chicago Blackhawks and Montreal Maroons in the playoffs to reach the best-of-five 1932 Stanley Cup Finals. Toronto won its third Cup in dominant fashion, sweeping the New York Rangers.

The feat would not be easily repeated. The Leafs reached the Finals in six of the next eight seasons but came up short every time. During those years of frustration, Toronto's roster included some of the biggest names in hockey. Conacher led the league in points in 1933–34 and 1934–35; center Syl Apps won the Calder Trophy as Rookie of the Year in 1936–37; and wing Gordie Drillon led all NHL players in scoring in 1937–38. In 1940, Day, who had retired as a player in 1938, replaced Irvin as the Maple Leafs' coach.

Maple Leafs Style

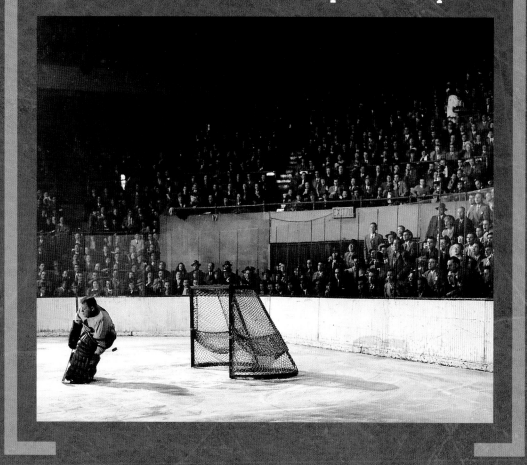

CONN SMYTHE, THE MAPLE LEAFS' SHREWD and legendary founder and longtime owner, wanted Maple Leafs games to be important social occasions in Toronto. Professional hockey was known as a tough, hard-hitting sport that often involved fistfights, but Smythe wanted to attract the "right" kind of crowd to Maple Leaf Gardens. So he decided that the arena's red seats—the most expensive ones, closest to the ice—would have special entrances, usherettes, and cushions. They would also have something else that made them uncommon: a dress code. Men sitting there had to wear ties and suits or sport coats, and women were required to wear dresses. If someone in those seats wasn't dressed appropriately, Smythe had a letter sent to the seat's ticket holder reminding him or her of the policy. The code was enforced for nearly 30 years, until the early 1960s, and no one seemed to mind. In fact, the elegance was often noted in the press, giving Maple Leafs games the increased social status Smythe had hoped for. Maple Leafs games at the Gardens were sellouts from 1946 to 1999, with season tickets being held by some of Toronto's best-known families for generations.

SUCCESS BY DAY

IN DAY'S FIRST SEASON AS COACH, GOALIE
Walter "Turk" Broda won the Vezina Trophy as the
league's best netminder, but the Leafs were quickly
eliminated in the playoffs. In 1941–42, Toronto finished 27–18–3 and advanced to the Stanley Cup
Finals, where it confronted the Detroit Red Wings.

After Toronto lost the series' first three games,
Day tried to inspire his players by reading them a
letter he said had been written by a 14-year-old
fan named Doris Klein. When the coach finished
the letter, which urged the Leafs to play with pride
and never give up, wing Sweeney Schriner jumped
to his feet. "Don't worry about this one, Skipper,"
he said. "We'll win it for the little girl."

Many people believe Coach Day manufactured
the letter himself, but regardless, the ploy worked.
The Leafs won not only Game 4, but four games in
a row, charging back to win the Stanley Cup in the

rence "Hap" (short for "Happy") Day was a natural leader who served the Maple Leafs as team captain for 10 seasons and then coach for 10 more.

greatest comeback in the history of pro sports. "It's the most amazing thing I've ever been a part of," said Drillon. "We just wouldn't quit."

Between 1939 and 1945, many NHL players put their skates away to fight in World War II. Apps and Broda were among them; even Smythe, who was then close to 50 years old, was wounded fighting in France. During these years, the NHL came to consist of just six teams: the Maple Leafs, the Montreal Canadiens, the Detroit Red Wings, the New York Rangers, the Chicago Blackhawks, and the Boston Bruins. These six teams would make up the NHL for the next 25 years.

Toronto suffered quick playoff defeats in 1943 and 1944. But assistant general manager Frank Selke picked up three key players during those years: defenseman Babe Pratt, center Ted Kennedy, and goalie Frank McCool. Pratt was a natural team leader who won the Hart Trophy as the league's Most

Charlie Conacher WING

Armed with one of the most powerful slap shots of his era, Charlie "The Big Bomber" Conacher was part of the Maple Leafs' "Kid Line" (along with wing Harvey "Busher" Jackson and center Joe Primeau) that made the Leafs a force in the 1930s. Conacher either led the league or tied for the lead in goals scored five times between 1930 and 1936, and his six playoff goals in 1932 carried the team to the Stanley Cup. He played against his older brother Lionel, a Montreal Maroons defenseman, in the Stanley Cup semifinals in 1932 and in the Finals in 1935.

MAPLE LEAFS SEASONS: 1929–38
HEIGHT: 6-0 (183 cm)
WEIGHT: 210 (95 kg)

- Career-high 36 goals in 1934–35
- 5-time All-Star
- 225 career goals
- Hockey Hall of Fame inductee (1961)

Ted Kennedy (left), Turk Broda (middle), and Syl Apps (right) all became Maple Leafs legends, winning two Stanley Cups together in the late 1940s.

Valuable Player (MVP) in 1943–44, and Kennedy (known to teammates and fans as "Teeder") was a tireless skater whom Conn Smythe called "the greatest competitor in hockey." McCool won the Calder Trophy as Rookie of the Year after the 1944–45 season, and his performance only improved in the 1945 playoffs. The Leafs knocked out heavily favored Montreal in six games in the semifinals and advanced to face their old nemesis, the Detroit Red Wings, in the Cup Finals.

McCool, who had so many stomach problems that he was nicknamed "Ulcers," set an NHL record by shutting out the Wings in the first three games. But Detroit stormed back to win the next three, threatening to repay the Leafs for the stunning comeback they'd carried off at the Wings' expense only three years before.

Game 7 was a nail-biter that was tied 1–1 in the third period. On a power play, the Leafs peppered Red Wings goalie Harry Lumley with four rapid shots before the puck went bouncing away. Then Pratt swooped in from near the blue line and slapped the loose puck into the net, giving the Leafs their second Stanley Cup in four years.

After the war ended, Apps and Broda returned, but the team seemed to have lost its winning chemistry. Pratt was suspended for gambling on hockey games in 1946, and the Leafs finished fifth out of the NHL's six teams. In a humbling turn of events, Toronto became only the second defending Stanley Cup winner ever to miss the playoffs.

Forty-Eight Legends

GREAT PLAYERS WHO HAVE WORN THE blue and white of the Toronto Maple Leafs haven't had to travel far to the Hockey Hall of Fame. It's right in downtown Toronto. Forty-eight former Toronto players are enshrined there today, second only to the 52 Montreal Canadiens greats who have been so honored. Although the Hall of Fame honored its first class of players in 1945, it wasn't until 1958 that the first Maple Leafs star was inducted. That star was Francis "King" Clancy, a defenseman on the 1932 Stanley Cup championship team. Three more Maple Leafs legends—Syl Apps, Hap Day, and Charlie Conacher, all of whom played on Cup winners—were inducted in 1961. Eleven Toronto coaches and executives, including both Conn Smythe and Harold Ballard, and even longtime broadcaster Foster Hewitt, are also in the Hall of Fame. Wing Dick Duff, who played until 1964, entered the Hall in 2006, and center Ron Francis went in in 2007. But the elegant building, formerly a bank, on the corner of Toronto's Front and Yonge Streets is almost certainly getting a spot ready for center Mats Sundin, who will likely retire as the club's all-time leading scorer.

A POSTWAR THREE-PEAT

THE 1946–47 MAPLE LEAFS WERE DETERMINED to prove that the previous season's stumble had been a fluke, and they did just that. The Leafs scored an NHL-high 209 goals and surged to the Stanley Cup Finals, where they faced Montreal. The Leafs were thrashed 6–0 in Game 1, and the next day's newspapers featured quotes from Canadiens goalie Bill Durnan questioning the Maple Leafs' talent. The public display of disrespect inspired the Leafs, who came back to topple their rivals in six games.

18

MAPLE LEAFS

The Maple Leafs (in white) were an NHL power in the late 1940s; in 1947–48, they lost just three home games, setting a club record that still stands.

In November 1947, the Leafs began their Cup defense with six straight wins, but Smythe wasn't satisfied. So he traded five players to Chicago for Max Bentley, who had led the league in scoring the previous two seasons. With Bentley aboard, the Maple Leafs finished the regular season atop the NHL, and Apps scored a hat trick on the final day of his final season, finishing with 201 goals for his career. "Two hundred goals wasn't bad in the 1940s," Apps would say years later. "Now everybody gets 200."

With a roster that featured such stars as Apps, Bentley, Kennedy, and Broda, the 1947–48 Leafs were arguably the greatest Toronto team ever assembled, and they breezed to the Stanley Cup. They topped the Boston Bruins in the postseason semifinals, four games to one, then swept Detroit in the Cup Finals.

Frank Mahovlich WING

At age 19, Frank Mahovlich was named the 1957–58 NHL Rookie of the Year, beating out Chicago Blackhawks star Bobby Hull for the honor. "The Big M" was the leading goal scorer on three of the four Stanley Cup-winning Leafs teams for which he played. But he couldn't seem to please fans or Toronto coach Punch Imlach, and the stress contributed to depression. Mahovlich was traded to the Detroit Red Wings in 1968, and he later led the Montreal Canadiens to two Stanley Cups. He was elected to the Hockey Hall of Fame in 1981 and in 1988 was appointed to the Canadian Senate.

MAPLE LEAFS SEASONS: 1956–68
HEIGHT: 6-0 (183 cm)
WEIGHT: 205 (93 kg)

- 1958 Calder Trophy winner (as Rookie of the Year)
- Career-high 49 goals in 1968–69
- 533 career goals
- 9-time All-Star

The Maple Leafs clashed with—and toppled—their close neighbors, the Detroit Red Wings, in the Stanley Cup Finals in 1945, 1948, and 1949.

The talented Leafs seemed to sleepwalk through the next season, finishing fourth. Then, when the playoffs began, they woke up. They beat Boston again in the semifinals, then squared off against Detroit again in the Finals. In Game 2, Toronto wing Sid Smith scored three power-play goals, tying an NHL record. The Leafs won that game and the next two, squashing the Red Wings with another sweep. Toronto's eighth world championship was a historic one, as it made the Leafs the first NHL team ever to win three Stanley Cups in a row.

In 1950, former Leafs center Joe Primeau replaced Hap Day as coach. With goalie Al Rollins splitting time in the nets with Broda and going 27–5–8 to win the Vezina Trophy, the Leafs advanced to the 1951 Cup Finals. Toronto won three of the first four games against Montreal, but Game 5 went into overtime. Three minutes into the extra session, in one of the most memorable moments in Toronto history, defenseman Bill Barilko took a diving leap at the puck and fired a shot past Canadiens goalie Gerry McNeil to win the Cup.

As Leafs fans soon came to discover, Barilko's thrilling goal represented the last hurrah in Toronto's run of dominance. New goalie Harry Lumley won the Vezina Trophy in 1953–54, and Kennedy won a long-overdue Hart Trophy in 1954–55. But between 1951 and 1958, the Leafs missed the playoffs three times and finished in last place once. Then Punch Imlach stepped in to turn things back around.

From Triumph to Tragedy

MAPLE LEAFS DEFENSEMAN BILL BARILKO was at the peak of his career during the 1950–51 season. In five seasons with Toronto, he had already skated as a top defenseman on three Stanley Cup-winning teams. And in April 1951, he was in the Cup Finals again as the Leafs took on the Montreal Canadiens. The first four games all went into overtime, with Toronto winning three of them. Game 5 was also tied at the end of regulation. Three minutes into overtime, Barilko—who, as a defenseman, wasn't expected to help much offensively—raced into the Montreal end to support a scramble behind the Canadiens' net. When the puck popped toward him, Barilko lunged and took a flying swipe at it from the left face-off circle, falling to the ice as the puck slipped past Montreal goalie Gerry McNeil, giving the Leafs their fifth Stanley Cup in seven seasons. That August, Barilko was flying home to Timmins, Ontario, from a fishing trip. The plane vanished, and the wreckage wasn't found until another pilot spotted it 11 years later, about 60 miles (97 km) north of Timmins. Barilko's Cup-winning goal had been the last shot of his life.

Imlach, a Toronto native and longtime minor-league coach, was hired as general manager by the Leafs in 1958. But after the team won only 5 of its first 16 games, he named himself coach and vowed that the Leafs would make the playoffs. They did that and more, reaching the 1959 Stanley Cup Finals before falling to Montreal in five games. Although he would eventually win four Stanley Cups with the Leafs, Imlach later called that improbable 1959 run "the greatest thrill of my life."

"I'm not here to win a popularity contest with the owners and the players. I'm here to win the Stanley Cup."

TORONTO COACH PUNCH IMLACH

24

MAPLE LEAFS

In the best season (1953–54) of his two-decade NHL career, Harry Lumley posted 13 shutouts, setting an NHL record that would stand for 16 years.

BACK TO THE TOP

IMLACH'S MAPLE LEAFS SQUADS OF THE LATE 1950s and early '60s featured some sensational players. Tall and graceful wing Frank Mahovlich had earned Rookie of the Year honors in 1957–58, and Imlach obtained former Detroit Red Wings star Red Kelly, a tough but classy center, in February 1960. The Leafs reached the 1960 Cup Finals, only to be swept by rival Montreal.

The next season, Conn Smythe sold his interest in the Maple Leafs to his son, Stafford, and an associate named Harold Ballard. Their reign would be long and would inspire bitterness in many players and fans due to bad business decisions and outright criminal behavior, but it could hardly have started better. In 1960–61, center Dave Keon won the Calder

Frank Mahovlich brought size, style, and a rare scoring touch to the Maple Leafs, but his relationship with the Toronto faithful was often strained.

Trophy, launching a Leafs career in which he would score 365 goals—the second-most in team history. Mahovlich scored 48 goals that season, and fearless goalie Johnny Bower won the Vezina Trophy. Detroit upset Toronto in the playoffs, but the Maple Leafs were back in contention.

After going 37–22–11 in 1961–62, the Leafs beat the New York Rangers in the semifinals and met the resurgent Chicago Blackhawks in the Cup Finals. The Leafs held a three-games-to-two series lead when Game 6 went into the third period with no score. Chicago's high-scoring wing, Bobby Hull, netted a goal in the third period, and fans in Chicago Stadium celebrated by pelting the ice with debris. But the 15-minute delay required to clean up the rink gave the Maple Leafs time to regroup. Toronto needed just 93 seconds to retie the score on a goal by wing Bob Nevin, and fellow Leafs wing Dick Duff scored the Cup winner four minutes after that.

Tim Horton DEFENSEMAN

Tim Horton may be best known today for the chain of coffee and donut shops that bear his name and are found along highways all across Canada. But he's almost as well known as one of the hardest-hitting defensemen ever to skate in the NHL. The tough but cool-headed Horton played on four Stanley Cup winners for Toronto in the 1960s. His NHL career spanned 24 seasons, including 20 with Toronto, where he was once 16 years older than the next-oldest defenseman. He played until he was 44, when he was killed in a car crash between Toronto and Buffalo, New York, driving home from a game.

MAPLE LEAFS SEASONS: 1951–70
HEIGHT: 5-10 (178 cm)
WEIGHT: 180 (82 kg)

- Career-high 12 goals in 1964–65
- 518 career points
- 6-time All-Star
- Hockey Hall of Fame inductee (1977)

Johnny Bower (right) was known for his aggression, often using the "poke check" technique of diving toward attacking players to stop the puck.

In 1962–63, the Leafs rolled to another Stanley Cup championship, losing only two games in the playoffs. The star of that postseason was Keon, who set an NHL record by scoring two shorthanded goals in the Cup-clinching game. "Frank Mahovlich might have been the engine of the Leafs in the 1960s," Conn Smythe once said, "but Davey was our spark plug. Without him, the engine wouldn't run."

> "I just made up my mind that I was going to lose my teeth and have my face cut to pieces."
>
> TORONTO GOALTENDER JOHNNY BOWER,
> ON BECOMING A GOALIE

The 1963–64 Leafs made history by securing Toronto's second "three-peat," but the players paid a high price in pain. In the 1964 Finals against the Red Wings, Toronto defenseman Bobby Baun broke his ankle stopping a shot in Game 6 but still scored the game winner in overtime. In Game 7, Leafs defenseman Carl Brewer played with separated ribs, wing and team captain George Armstrong skated with a separated shoulder, and Kelly played on damaged knee ligaments. Their toughness was rewarded, as the Leafs won the game and series 4–0. Kelly left Maple Leaf Gardens in an ambulance, and Baun left on crutches.

The Harold Ballard Blues

IN NOVEMBER 1961, LONGTIME TEAM owner Conn Smythe sold his interest in the Maple Leafs and Maple Leaf Gardens to his son, Stafford, and to Harold Ballard, who had worked his way into the Leafs organization through the minor-league Toronto Marlboros. The Maple Leafs won four more Stanley Cups in the next six seasons, but a long slide in their reputation and traditions was beginning. First, the two new partners got caught up in financial crimes, including fraud, theft, and tax evasion. After Stafford Smythe died in 1971, Ballard bought his shares, but he was soon sentenced to prison. Returning to the team while on parole in 1973, Ballard implemented numerous Gardens changes intended to increase profits. He narrowed the seats, posted advertisements, and ended the dress code in the expensive seats. Ballard also cut back on the team's scouting budget, battled with the new players' union, and—in the span of 7 seasons in the 1970s—lost 18 players to better salary offers from the competing World Hockey Association. The Leafs went through eight coaches between 1977 and 1990 (the year that Ballard died) and never finished better than third in their division between 1967 and 1999.

The next year, Bower and veteran goalie Terry Sawchuk shared the Vezina Trophy, but it was the first of two mediocre seasons for the Leafs. By the time the 1967 playoffs rolled around, the Leafs were an old team. Bower was 42, Kelly 39, Sawchuk 37, defenseman Tim Horton 37, and Armstrong 36. This graying group proved it wasn't washed up yet, though, topping Montreal in six games to win the Cup. After the championship-clinching game, Sawchuk skipped the on-ice celebration. "I don't like Champagne," he said, "and I'm too tired to dance around."

"He was the best coach I ever saw. He was like a mind reader."

MAPLE LEAFS OWNER CONN SMYTHE, ON PUNCH IMLACH

Toronto was king of the hockey world for the 13th time, but its dynasty was about to crumble. Mahovlich had led the Leafs in goals in three of their four Cup-winning seasons in the 1960s, but he feuded with Coach Imlach and would be traded to Detroit in 1968. Many of the team's other stars had finally grown old. The NHL doubled in size to 12 teams before the 1967–68 season, and the Leafs settled into the back of the pack. The glory days were over in Toronto.

one of the final highlights of his great career, Terry Sawchuk gave up just one goal in the last, championship-clinching game of the 1967 Cup Finals.

STARS IN THE DARK YEARS

EVEN AS THE MAPLE LEAFS DECLINED IN THE standings, Toronto fans found reasons to cheer. Center Darryl Sittler, defenseman Borje Salming, and wing Lanny McDonald entertained the crowds in the Gardens throughout the 1970s. Sittler was a natural leader who would become the Leafs' all-time leading scorer, while Salming, signed out of Sweden in 1973, would set the franchise assist record (620) over the course of his 16 seasons in Toronto.

"It must be spring. The Leafs are out."

TORONTO SUN EDITORIAL, ON THE MAPLE LEAFS MISSING THE PLAYOFFS AGAIN IN THE 1980S

34

MAPLE LEAFS

A team captain by age 25 and one of the most popular Maple Leafs stars ever, Darryl Sittler was famous for his ability to score in flurries.

McDonald was a feisty, mustachioed forward who spent seven seasons in Toronto and led the team in goals three times. He and Sittler formed such a potent and close pair that when owner Harold Ballard traded McDonald to the Colorado Rockies in late 1979, Sittler took a scissors and cut the captain's "C" off of his sweater in protest. Sittler himself was soon traded to Philadelphia.

Wing Rick Vaive provided most of the Leafs' offensive firepower in the 1980s, using a booming slap shot to score a team-record 54 goals in 1981–82. Scrappy wing Wendel Clark also became a fan favorite with his thunderous body checks in the mid-1980s. But such individual heroics aside, the decade was a dismal one for Toronto. From 1979–80 to 1991–92, the Leafs would lose more games than they won every year but one, when they merely broke even. That season, 1989–90, it took 51 goals by wing Gary Leeman to muster a 38–38–4 record.

Borje Salming DEFENSEMAN

Borje Salming was one of the first Swedes to play in the NHL, and his impact didn't stop there. The defenseman was also the first Swede to be inducted into the Hockey Hall of Fame. "For us Swedish hockey players, he is the man who showed us the right way," Maple Leafs center Mats Sundin once said. "He is a trailblazer." Salming's misfortune was his timing; the Maple Leafs' best showings in his 16 seasons were several third-place divisional finishes and one conference semifinals appearance. After retiring from hockey, Salming ran a clothing factory and a brewery in Sweden.

MAPLE LEAFS SEASONS: 1973–89
HEIGHT: 6-1 (180 cm)
WEIGHT: 185 (84 kg)

- 787 career points
- Career-high 19 goals in 1979–80
- 6-time All-Star
- Hockey Hall of Fame inductee (1996)

Both scrappy and accurate, Rick Vaive was an offensive machine, breaking the prestigious 50-goal mark in three seasons in the early 1980s.

Harold Ballard died in 1990, and Toronto businessman Steve Stavro soon took control of the team. In 1992–93, defenseman Doug Gilmour set team records for assists (95) and points (127) in a season. Along with big wing Dave Andreychuk, a midseason acquisition, Gilmour powered the Leafs to the 1993 Campbell Conference Finals. The Leafs would go no farther, though, losing to the Los Angeles Kings and their star center, Wayne Gretzky, in seven games. The Leafs made the 1994 conference finals as well but again fell short, this time losing to the Vancouver Canucks.

After that loss, the Leafs traded Clark to the Quebec Nordiques for center Mats Sundin, who would go on to lead the Leafs in scoring for 10 of the next 11 seasons. Beginning in 1998–99, Toronto emerged as one of the NHL's most consistently formidable teams, reeling off 7 seasons of 40 or more wins over the next 8 years. In 1999–2000, Sundin and goalie Curtis Joseph helped the Leafs win the Northeast Division of the Eastern Conference (the NHL had been split into Eastern and Western Conferences in 1993), giving them their first regular-season first-place finish in 37 years. In 2002, they returned to the Eastern Conference Finals but were denied a Stanley Cup Finals berth by the Carolina Hurricanes.

"Rick is one tough guy. A lot of guys thought they could take him. A lot of guys were wrong."

TORONTO DEFENSEMAN BOB MCGILL,
ON RICK VAIVE'S FIGHTING ABILITY

The 50-Goal Club

Dave Andreychuk

ALTHOUGH WING MAURICE "ROCKET" RICHARD of Toronto's rival, the Montreal Canadiens, was the first player in the NHL to score 50 goals in a season (in 1944–45), it wasn't until 1982 that a Maple Leafs player broke that prestigious mark. Some great players came close. Hall-of-Famer Frank Mahovlich, who led the Leafs in goals for six straight seasons, scored 48 in 1960–61, going scoreless in his final 14 games. (By then, teams were playing 70 games in a season, whereas Richard scored his 50 goals in 50 games.) Lanny McDonald netted 47 during the 1977–78 season, the same year the great Darryl Sittler had 45. Sittler, the Leafs' all-time scoring leader, netted more than 40 goals in 4 different seasons. But the man who finally broke the barrier was wing Rick Vaive. In 1981–82, his third season with Toronto, Vaive "lit the lamp" 54 times. He scored 51 the next season and 52 the year after that, but his 54-goal season remains the franchise record. Two other Leafs players have scored more than 50 goals in a season since Vaive: Gary Leeman (with 51 in 1989–90) and Dave Andreychuk (with 53 in 1993–94).

The next two years, the Leafs looked strong during the regular season but lost early in the playoffs. Then, after the 2004–05 season was cancelled due to a salary dispute between owners and players, Toronto dropped in the standings, missing the 2006 and 2007 playoffs. The main problem was that the team had gotten old. Sundin was still a dangerous scorer, but other veterans—such as longtime wing Tie Domi and former All-Star goalie Ed Belfour—were nearing retirement.

In 2007, Toronto marked the 40th anniversary of its last Stanley Cup championship by publishing an open letter to Maple Leafs fans thanking them for their support during the long drought and promising improvements. Many Leafs players and fans, including Mats Sundin, were encouraged by the potential of such rising talents as center Nik Antropov and wing Alex Steen. "All I want to do is win a championship," said Sundin, "and I want to win a Stanley Cup."

Walter "Turk" Broda GOALIE

Turk Broda was a fan favorite due to his fun-loving attitude, portly appearance, and durability. He tended the nets for five Stanley Cup-winning Maple Leafs teams from 1942 through 1951 (missing two seasons while serving in World War II) and is still the team's career leader in shutouts and games won and lost. Broda often struggled to keep his weight in check but won the Vezina Trophy as the league's top goalie in 1941 and 1948 and produced 13 playoff shutouts in his career—three of them in 1950 in the only playoff games the Leafs won that year.

MAPLE LEAFS SEASONS: 1936–43, 1945–52
HEIGHT: 5-9 (175 cm)
WEIGHT: 185 (84 kg)

- 3-time All-Star
- 1.98 career playoff goals-against average (GAA)
- Team-record 62 career shutouts
- Hockey Hall of Fame inductee (1967)

Longtime Leafs wing Tie Domi was an unremarkable scorer and passer but was a feared enforcer who was notorious for his willingness to fight.

As they carry on a tradition that includes 13 Stanley Cups and an all-time roster that features such legendary names as Hap Day, Ted Kennedy, and Darryl Sittler, today's Maple Leafs players have a lot to live up to. The Stanley Cup has eluded the Leafs since 1967, but a new generation of Leafs—proudly bearing the symbol of Canada on their blue and white sweaters, and spurred on by the cheers of some of the world's most passionate fans—is hoping to make Toronto the hockey capital of the world once again.

"This is a beautiful building. But I think we will all leave a little piece of ourselves at the Gardens."

TORONTO CENTER MATS SUNDIN,
ON MOVING OUT OF MAPLE LEAF GARDENS
AND INTO THE AIR CANADA CENTRE

42

MAPLE LEAFS

BUILT IN LESS THAN SIX MONTHS AT A cost of $1.5 million during the Great Depression, Maple Leaf Gardens opened on November 12, 1931, with the Leafs losing to the Chicago Blackhawks, 2–1. Despite that beginning, the Gardens provided a long-term home-ice advantage for the Leafs, who would win 11 Stanley Cups in 68 years there. In the 1960s, the Gardens also hosted concerts by such legendary performers as Elvis Presley and the Beatles. But by the '90s, the arena was considered too small to be profitable for sports teams and event promoters. The National Basketball Association's Toronto Raptors, who had been playing at the Gardens since 1995, started building their own arena about a mile away, near the city's lakefront. Owners of the Leafs and Maple Leaf Gardens then bought the Raptors and the new, $265-million Air Canada Centre (ACC), which was redesigned to accommodate a hockey rink. In February 1999, both teams played their first games in the ACC. The arena boasts three restaurants and themed concession stands, and hockey fans can practice their own slap shots in an interactive attraction called the Fan Zone. The Leafs seem to like the new arena: they've compiled a winning record every season since moving in.

Young center Kyle Wellwood and the Maple Leafs entertained crowds in the Air Canada Centre in 2006–07 but missed the playoffs by a mere point.

Punch Imlach COACH

George Imlach came by his nickname honestly. After being knocked "punchy," or dizzy, by a hard check while playing in a minor-league game, he was known for the rest of his life as "Punch." Imlach became one of the shrewdest and most successful coaches and executives in Maple Leafs history. Known for his heavy-handed practices and strict personality, Imlach alienated some star players; defenseman Carl Brewer quit the team in 1965 after a locker room argument with Imlach. But many others were loyal. After Imlach was fired in 1969, defenseman Tim Horton considered retiring, saying, "If this team doesn't want Imlach, I guess it doesn't want me."

MAPLE LEAFS SEASONS AS COACH: 1958–69, 1979–80
NHL COACHING RECORD: 423–373–163
STANLEY CUP CHAMPIONSHIPS WITH TORONTO: 1962, 1963, 1964, 1967
HOCKEY HALL OF FAME INDUCTEE (1984)

MAPLE LEAFS